# YOUR KNOWLEDGE HAS

**Malko Ebers**

# Shrinking cities, the hidden challenge

GRIN Verlag

**Bibliografische Information der Deutschen Nationalbibliothek:**

Die Deutsche Bibliothek verzeichnet diese Publikation in der Deutschen National-
bibliografie; detaillierte bibliografische Daten sind im Internet über http://dnb.d-
nb.de/ abrufbar.

**Imprint:**

Copyright © 2005 GRIN Verlag GmbH
Druck und Bindung: Books on Demand GmbH, Norderstedt Germany
ISBN: 978-3-638-65119-6

**This book at GRIN:**

http://www.grin.com/en/e-book/52635/shrinking-cities-the-hidden-challenge

**Yale University – Fall 2005**
School of Management
Course: Management of Global Cities

**Malko Ebers**

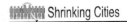 Shrinking Cities

# Contents

1. Introduction   2

2. Growth and decline of cities   3

   2.1.  The conditions for city growth and decline   4
   2.2.  Time, space and city development   7
   2.3.  Shrinkage and the death of public sphere   11

3. Cities with a past but no future?   13

   3.1.  Shrinking industries - Detroit is not alone   14
   3.2.  The East German case   16

4. What can be done?   18

5. Concluding Remarks   22

*References*

*Annex*

A1: Annual growth rate of global population
A2: Percent aged 65 and over
A3: The World's 25 oldest countries 2000
A4: Fertility rate in the EU-25
A5: Eurostat: Annual average population change 1996-2001
A6: Population dynamics of broad age groups in East Germany

## 1. Introduction

The story of world demographics is a growth story and it is very closely linked to urbanization. Since the early 19th century population growth has accelerated dramatically. 118 years, this is the time it took to increase world population from one billion in 1807 to two billion. For the third billion reached in 1922 only 37 years were necessary and the jump from 5 to over 6 billion world population was done in an un-preceded 12 years[1]. The increase in world population has influenced many observers to use terms such as 'explosion' or 'over-population' and 'mega-cities'. Indeed the growth patterns are very closely linked to a sustainable trend towards higher levels of urbanization. As UN data shows 3 billion people are already living in cities. This trend is continuing leading to 5 billion city dwellers by 2030 and the percentage of world population living in cities is expected to pass 50 per cent in 2007[2].

In the public and also academic discussion of urbanization and world demographic trends, cities such as Lagos, Nairobi, Karachi, Dhaka or Mumbai are often the case studies for the enormous challenges growing cities have to deal with. These challenges have to do with growing scarcity of resources, collapse of infrastructure, poverty and environmental problems.

Although population growth and the challenges it presents for cities, mostly in the developing world, is a very serious issue, there is another topic deserving attention. Overall city populations are increasing but there is no single trend as there is no single city. Growth patterns vary very significantly between cities, countries and even continents. African cities such as Lagos and several Asian cities such as Bejing or Shanghai are expected to grow steadily at least for the next decades, whereas several cities in the Western world already show signs of decline and shrinkage. Former industrial centers such as Detroit, Pittsburgh or Manchester suffering from the economic shift towards a modern service industry are not alone. According to the Berkeley Institute of Urban and Regional Development: *"Today, every 6th city in the world can be defined as a "shrinking city".*"[3].

---

[1] U.S. Census Bureau (2004): 1. As annex 1 shows the speed of population growth slowed down after 1999 so that world population will be growing but it will also be aging at a higher rate.
[2] UN Press Release (2004)
[3] Berkeley (2005): http://www-iurd.ced.berkeley.edu/scg/index.htm. Since empirical comparative data on shrinking cities is very seldom these results/statements should be interpreted carefully.

This paper aims at casting light on the hidden challenge of shrinking cities. Its main hypothesis is that in the current debate on the effects of demographic change and city management shrinking cities are widely neglected but will be a major urbanization issue in the near future.

The first part 'Growth and decline of cities' presents and discusses world urbanization trends. Hereby the idea is to contrast trends of growing urbanization and population increase with the spreading phenomenon of shrinking cities. Furthermore the conditions for the rise and decline of cities are identified. Based on this more introductory part, 'Cities with a past but no future?' focuses on case studies of city shrinkage. Among the most often found cases in the literature are cities such as Detroit, Manchester and East German cities.

## 2. Growth and decline of cities

As already pointed out 2007 will most probably be the first year in human history that

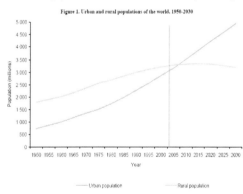

Figure 1. Urban and rural populations of the world, 1950-2030

more people will be living in cities than in rural areas. As the graphic on the left shows this trend is going to continue. Nevertheless it shouldn't be overseen that the already high number of shrinking cities will increase too. Besides very clear cases of growing (mega-) cities (above 5 million inhabitants) such as Lagos growing from 12 million in 2003 to about 24 million 2015 and declining cities such as Hoyerswerda in East Germany there will be several mixed types where growth and shrinking happens simultaneously in different areas of the same city: *"Until today we have planned cities for growth, but we must also plan for their decline."*[4].

---

[4] Holcim Foundation (2005): 158

Mega-cities get the highest public attention in this growth process: *"Yet, despite their size and importance, mega-cities still account for only a small share of the world's urban population and of course of the world's total population."*[5]. Even though the number of mega-cities is expected to increase significantly by 2015 they will account 'only' for 5% of world population compared to 4,1% in 2000[6].

In the long run- according to U.S. Census Bureau data *"the level of fertility for the world as a whole will drop below replacement level before 2050."*[7]. But already today and in the foreseeable future shrinking populations and in turn shrinking cities play an important role. The continuous population growth (at least until 2050) is very unevenly distributed. Africa and Asia are the present and future growth centers, also with the highest increase in urbanization levels, whereas for example Europe, Argentina, Australia and to a lower degree the US will have stagnating or declining populations[8]. These patterns will be discussed in more detail in part 2.1. *Time, space and city development.*

The following two points present the conditions that favor city growth or lead to its decline. There is no single variable that explains the rise and shrinkage of cities; nevertheless it should be possible to determine the most important influence factors of city development.

## 2.1. The conditions of city growth and decline

The rise and fall of Rome is an expression everybody knows. Lost cities have been found in Middle-America centuries after their inhabitants left them, volcanism wiped out Pompeii and war destroyed cities from ancient Cartage to Nagasaki in World War Two. Natural catastrophes such as recently the Tsunami in East Asia, hurricanes Rita and Katrina flooding New Orleans, earth quakes in Kobe, Japan or Pakistan will always severely affect cities and are hard to calculate.

---

[5] ECOSOC (2004): 84, see also: Cohen, B. (2004)
[6] See: ECOSOC (2004): 84
[7] U.S. Census (2004): 2. Such an estimate should of course be interpreted carefully, since there are numerous influence factors of population growth ranging from economic prosperity over the AIDS pandemic to natural catastrophes and warfare.
[8] ECOSOC (2004): 1-3

4

Besides natural catastrophes, war destruction and other relatively seldom, single events there are less spectacular factors that lead to city shrinkage and general decline. Economic or demographic changes are powerful but very silent factors that usually need decades to be significantly felt by city inhabitants. Usually these factors impact cities in whole regions such as for example the formerly industrialized rust belt in the US or the "Ruhrgebiet" in West Germany. Scarcity of resources, of labor and especially capital might lead to a vicious circle. When city economies focus on a few goods and industries they might grow at a very rapid rate. This was the case for Manchester focusing on textiles and for Detroit relying heavily on the automotive sector. A supply industry develops, whole areas of the city become neighborhoods for workers of very few factories and the sector continues to specialize. As long as the industry performs well, the city as a whole, its tax base, infrastructure and cultural life is prosperous. When the national economy changes in an unfavorable way for the city's economy the reason for its rapid growth becomes the main factor for its rapid decline. Technological change, high competition or the collapse of (overseas) markets or supply can be seen as at the core of the shrinkage, based on the assumption of competition between cities.

In very general terms resources enable city growth but also limit its scope. The size of ancient cities of Mesopotamia and other early settlements was determined by the availability and quality of its surrounding agriculture. Therefore historical cities can often be found at trade ways and rivers to secure sustainable food supply. As Lewis Mumford remarks: *"These early cities bore many marks of their village origins, for they were still in essence agricultural towns: [...] they could not grow beyond the limit of their local water supply and their local food sources."*[9].

Another characteristic of the early city was its high degree of autonomy and low interconnection with other cities. They were often religious and administrative centers, market places, protected by courts and law enforcement mechanisms, often surrounded by high walls against enemies. Over the course of history natural restrictions such as the quality and quantity of soil, became less and less relevant and finally vanished. On the one hand improvements in agricultural methods and technology increased efficiency and made cities more autonomous. On the other

---

[9] Mumford, L. (1956)

5

hand improvements in sea- and water transportation and communication systems dramatically improved the interconnection between cities and sustainable food and resource supply.

One can stress religion, centralized administration, the symbolic value of capitals and many other reasons for growth and decline of cities. Since not only but also through globalization cities are nowadays more interconnected than ever before in history I like to see current cities foremost as market places. The view of cities as marketplaces that secured economic exchange is of course not new and goes back to the earliest (urban) sociologists such as Georg Simmel (1905), Max Weber (1905) and others[10]. Two developments were and are still at work. The transaction costs of relocating capital have decreased and the opportunity costs for inhabitants to stay in a declining city are increasing. Investors nowadays have a higher opportunity to move (their capital, investments) to more productive places and so have city inhabitants. To explain the shrinkage of cities, (economic) utility maximization of city inhabitants, who choose between several competing cities is seen as the main condition for city growth. There is not only a growing mobility of inhabitants between cities but also within the city. Continuously declining commuter costs are among the main factors causing the growing trend of sub-urbanization and therefore declining density. Analyzing empirical data from a study done by Kim (2005) on *the rise and decline of U.S. urban densities*[11] helps to identify and to distinct the two trends of sub-urbanization and of shrinkage. The population density of cities increased since 1890 (7,203 inhabitants per square mile), peaked in 1950 with 8876 inhabitants per square mile and is declining since reaching 5647 in 1990 the most recent data entry of the study. This decline of around 36% since 1950 does not necessarily mean shrinkage of the overall city since the size of cities also grew and people might have moved to the suburbs. Therefore one would have to control for the population size of the whole metropolitan region. Putting together the two data tables of Kim for city and metropolitan region development shows that both trends were at work. City density declines by 36%-an estimate for sub-urbanization but also the whole metropolitan region lost inhabitants-an estimate for people leaving to other cities (shrinkage). Here

---

[10] For a detailed overview of Webers' conception see: Flanagan, W.G. (1990): 50
[11] Kim, S. (2005)

the density peaked in 1960 with 589,4 inhabitants per square mile and declined steadily reaching 288 in 1990, which means a 51% decrease over the observed time period[12].

## 2.2. Time, space and city development

This paragraph is about to show how city develop over time and how (population) growth centers and regions where cities shrink are distributed geographically. The following graphic[13] is taken from the ECOSOC Population Division *World Urbanization Prospects Report* and gives a first impression how urban and rural population growth varies over time.

One striking pattern is that the urban population in less developed countries will increase steadily and will make up the very biggest share of population growth in the future.

Figure 2. Contributions of urban and rural population growth to total population growth, 1950-2030

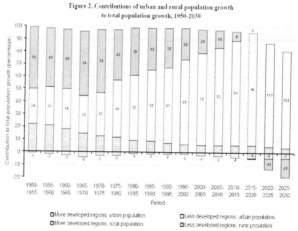

In the early 1950s the contribution of urban growth from less developed regions relatively to urban population growth from developed regions was 1,3 times bigger. Nowadays urban population growth from less developed countries is 12,7 times

---

[12] Se : Kim, S. (2005) : 15-16
[13] ECOSOC Population Division (2004): 10

bigger than the shrinking population growth in developed countries[14]. This huge gap between growing urban populations in less developed countries such as in Africa and very low growing or shrinking urban populations in developed nations such as in Europe is going to increase further. The gap widened in the mid 1970s and will steadily enlarge until 2020. Afterwards the gap will decrease just slightly due to increased aging processes in todays so called *youth bulge* countries of the third world. Given this data it comes therefore at no surprise that the phenomenon of shrinking cities is foremost a Western phenomenon. Dramatic economic changes in the Chinese economy, combined with the one-child policy leading to aging at high pace, will also bring the European and US phenomenon of shrinking cities to the Asian continent. Today shrinking cities are more related to economic changes and areas in Europe and the US than to Asia. But this is going to change when China and today's very young populations will be aging, partly declining in population size. It is therefore probable that demography will replace economic changes as the key variable influencing the size of cities. But besides vague estimates and hypotheses, how dramatic is the phenomenon of shrinking cities already?

The graphic[15] on the left might be a first guess for the high importance this phenomenon already has.

The graphic visualizes 1990-1999 growth data for US cities and shows which city's population increased and which declined. Given the New Economy boom for the 1990s there might be an underestimate for shrinking cities compared to other decades, but still, the decline of city population seems to be nearly as commonplace as city growth.

---

[14] Own calculation based on ECOSOC data. In: ECOSOC Population Division (2004): 10
[15] U.S. Census Bureau

Another striking characteristic is the regional distribution of growing and shrinking cities. Shrinking cities are particularly seldom in the highly New Economy driven so called sun-belt of California, but are noticeably often in the so called rust-belt with cities such as Pittsburgh or Detroit (marked with a red circle). This might be seen as another hint for the validity of the economic argument. Taking the assumption for granted that city governments have a disadvantage from shrinking cities (smaller tax-base etc.) and given the graphic data it is most plausible that cities compete for citizens. Adding today's relatively high mobility (low transaction costs) several cities decline economically, loose attractivity, in turn citizens, which in turn decreases their attractivity again.

Comparative (international) data on shrinking cities is rare but one study by Oswalt and Rienitz reports that between 1950 and 2000 at least 350 cities above 100,000 inhabitants had a population loss over 10%. During these 50 years the number of shrinking cities grew by 330% and: *"Researchers say shrinking cities outnumber growing cities – in spite of current and projected urban growth."*[16].

Classic examples for shrinking cities are from Europe. Especially UK's former industrial centers in the Midlands Liverpool and Manchester as well as several cities such as Halle and Leipzig in East Germany have shrunk significantly in the past decades: *"The shrinking city is a global phenomenon, and the shrinkage is greatest in Europe and the United States. The statistics presented by Philipp Oswalt and Tim Rieniets suggest that the trend will increase in the future because Europe will hardly contribute to world population growth."*[17]. Unfortunately there is not yet much academic research on shrinking cities and an Atlas of shrinking cities done by Oswalt and Rienitz was not yet published[18]. This paper summarizes some macro data for the US and parts of Europe, includes some data on international levels of urbanization and demographic trends but relies also strongly on case studies. As already pointed out the reasons for the shrinkage are numerous therefore one should be careful drawing conclusions from case studies. Nevertheless the author is of the opinion that Detroit and Manchester are good ideal types for economic and selected East German cities for political change and its impact on city life and growth.

[16] Holcim Foundation (2005): 158
[17] Holcim Foundation (2005): 159-160
[18] ib

A rough indicator where future shrinkage will be most common is demographic development. As Annex A2 and A3 show, Europe is already the oldest continent and from the 25 oldest countries in the world (measured as percentage of citizens over 65 years of age) only Japan is non-European. As Eurostat data shows, since 1975 European countries fail to achieve the value of 2,1 birth fertility rate, which would keep population size at its current rate. The problem of aging and most probably decreasing population size and therefore shrinking cities is nearly as high in countries such as Argentina, Australia, Russia and North America. Here the percentage of people over 65 years of age is already between 8 and 12,9% compared to over 13% for Europe. Demographic projections are often biased, but even in the case of increased immigration these countries will most probably have a demographic problem and city managers should prepare for aging inhabitants and problems of shrinkage. An analysis of US census data on city population size shows that cities, which shrink, do so over decades and turnarounds are very seldom[19]. It seems that shrinking cities exhibit a strong path dependency and are in most cases more object of economic transition than active creators of economic infrastructure and city growth.

A somehow typical growth and decline cycle represents New Orleans, suffering not only from the dangers of hurricanes and flooding but also from a very strong dependency on its harbor. The city of New Orleans is in the news today and its population might be cut in half after the post-hurricane reconstruction[20]. New Orleans is not only the example of our times how a single event can drastically shrink a city's population but also a typical example for silent decline. The former prosperous, major city of the South, reaching more than 700, 000 inhabitants at its height in 1965 declined continuously in the decades afterwards (see graphic on next page)[21].

After hurricanes Katrina and Rita hit, the current population is estimated at 150,000 and according to the city's administration the city won't fully recover and will have between 250,000 and 300,000 inhabitants after its reconstruction[22]. Damages

---

[19] Data taken from: Kingsley, G., Pettit, K. (2002)
[20] According to New Orleans mayor Nagin. In: Washington Post (2005)
[21] Table was calculated based on data taken from: Wikipedia (2005): New Orleans
[22] New Orleans Major Nagy in Washington Post (2005)

and a smaller tax base means in turn a decline of annual city budget from $600 to 230 million[23].

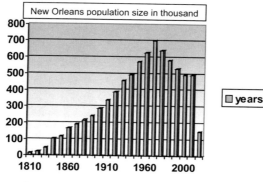

A catastrophe such as hurricane Katrina is of course among the most extreme causes of city shrinkage. But what are the effects of this on city life and is shrinkage at all negative or could it mean more resources for fewer people? These are the leading questions to be answered in the next paragraph.

## 2.3. Shrinkage and the death of public sphere

At first hand one might wonder what could be so negative about a shrinking city? Less people would use the existing infrastructure, from streets to parks, museums, pools and libraries. The mistake in this perspective is that a shrinking city is fundamentally different from just a small city. A change in quantity means also a change in quality and a fundamental impact on every day life. This statement becomes clearer by using a terminology developed by early urban sociologist Louis Wirth. In his famous article 'Urbanism as a way of life' (1938) Wirth proposed three criteria to analyze any city: the size of city population, population density and heterogeneity of the inhabitants[24]. Since then these three elements have become standards to describe cities. Wirth's criteria don't help us much in deciding how many inhabitants a settlement must have to speak of a city or how dense and heterogeneous it must be. Nevertheless these analytical criteria represent a simple, functional framework that allows us to identify a degree of urbanization and to compare (ideal typically) different settlements/cities according to these criteria. When

---

[23] Washington Post (2005)
[24] See: Flanagan, W. G. (1993): 16

11

a city's population shrinks, usually also the population density sinks. Furthermore the heterogeneity decreases since the most mobile, often young people move away searching for new jobs, better opportunities. Those who stay last are the immobile, elderly, the poor and disabled. Again, it is important to acknowledge that shrinking cities are not just like smaller cities. It is like someone's clothes have become too big, it just doesn't fit. A shrinking population and decreasing density leads to higher transaction and per unit costs of public services while at the same time the tax base shrinks. Public goods from parks, museums to streets become over dimensioned causing more costs than the shrinking tax base can afford. And increases in tax rate in turn accelerate the shrinkage process. One of the most visible indicator of shrinking cities are vacant buildings. In East Germany as a whole for example 1,3 million apartments are unattended and this figure is expected to increase to 2 million by 2030[25]. In parts of Detroit in the 1980s more than 40% of the buildings were abandoned, not surprisingly for a city that lost about 47% of its population since its height in the 1950s[26]. Other examples with very high vacancy rates and where *"unemployment soared to unimaginable heights"*[27] include Liverpool and Manchester among many, many others. Cities are not merely an agglomeration of buildings, factories and apartments, but diverse, complex social entities where culture and

public goods are created. When cities shrink and public goods such as cultural institutions, theatres, parks, museums, police and fire houses are in decline the city is reduced from a vital public place to a mere functional collection of people and buildings. Social life, the interaction of people besides their work, a major urban source of creativity and innovation comes to an end.

Social life usually shrinks at a similar or higher pace than the actual loss of citizens. The figure on the left *sole man* from Chicago symbolizes how the remaining citizens loose their institutions of interaction (public goods) and places where *the public* is socially created. Or similarly as Mitch Cope writing about the declining Detroit metropolitan area expresses it: *"It is like a dysfunctional family whose members*

---

[25] Shrinking Cities Project (2004)
[26] Mirel, J. (1998): 240
[27] Shrinking Cities (2004): 115

*refuse to talk to each other, all sharing the same toilet, the same lights, the same house, while each individual lives in his or her own isolated world*[28]. Shrinkage, unemployment, dying social life and increased crime are consequences that reinforce each other and can lead to a vicious circle.

 **3. Cities with a past but no future?**

Derived from the recent literature on city development chapter three discusses some of the most known examples for city shrinkage. By outlining the cases of Detroit, Manchester, Liverpool and East German cities such as Halle or Hoyerswerda the chapter discusses the question if there are cities with a past but no future? Are there typical patterns for growth and decline and what might be a lesson learned from this analysis?

Chapter two has presented more a macro perspective how, where and when shrinking processes occur and what possible explanations could be. Shrinkage and the death of public sphere were meant to be preparatory for this chapter. A kind of bridge from a more quantitative macro perspective to a more qualitative discussion of single cities and their experience with growth and decline patterns of their development. The final aim is to identify lessons learned from positive turnarounds such as in the case of Manchester, which can be generalized.

Over the course of history cities have done amazing reconstruction and turnarounds from shrinking and decline processes. San Francisco has recovered from the big earthquake in 1905, LA from a major earthquake in 1994 causing billions of damage. Berlin has been reconstructed and grown after nearly total devastation in the Second World War and even Hiroshima, albeit on a much smaller scale has grown again. It is interesting not only how the turnaround was possible, but also how these cities often looked differently afterwards, how they managed an often-smaller size and different structure. The mentioned examples are cases of single, extreme events such as war and forces of nature whereas socio-economic causes of decline usually take decades and might be a harder to manage, hidden threat for city planers.

---

[28] Cope, M. (2004). In Shrinking Cities (2004) Detroit: 11

## 3.1. Shrinking industries – Detroit is not alone

Detroit is not alone was the headline of a Detroit newspaper article reporting about a tremendous art project called shrinking cities[29]. This project involving around a hundred international researchers, architects and artists casts light on the relatively neglected phenomenon of shrinking cities. It puts the well-known example of Detroit into context by studying this city plus Manchester, Ivanovo in Russia, Leipzig and Halle in Germany as ideal types for international city shrinkage. It is very surprisingly that this phenomenon has not yet achieved much especially academic attention and this exhibition is helping to bridge the gap.

The reason that Detroit grew once so rapidly has become the explanation for its fast decline- high dependency on a single industry. The following statement from 2005 illustrates the enormous vacancy rate: *"A city the size of San Francisco could fit in the total area of Detroit's empty buildings and vacant lots."*[30].

What the motor industry has been for the *Motor city* and industrial powerhouse Detroit was the harbor for New Orleans, textiles for Manchester and coal for Hoyerswerda. New Orleans as well has been a shrinking city for decades. It declined by 10,8% from 1980 to 1990 and continued to decline by 2,5% until 1999[31], not to speak of hurricane Katrina. These are kind of typical patterns of population decline, which can be found in areas with a former high degree of industrialization. In the US this would be true for the so-called *rust belt* an area in the Northeast of the country with its characteristically focus on coal, steel and other heavy industries. The cities in this area were once among the fastest growing, largest and wealthiest in the nation: *"At the turn of the 20th Century until the Great Depression, Detroit experienced unparalleled growth through immigration. This growth was fueled by the jobs created by the automobile industry, as well as the images of a beautiful, treed city where home ownership was the highest in the nation and everyone had a car."*[32]. The growth patterns were additionally fueled by billions of dollars worth defense contracts during two World Wars and thereafter[33]. A quick look at US census data alone reveals that

---

[29] Collins, L. (2003)
[30] Vogel, S. (2005): 2
[31] Kingsley,G., Pettit,K. (2002)
[32] Vogel, S. (2005): 1
[33] See: Booza, J., Metzger, K. (2004). In: Shrinking Cities, Detroit (2004): 45

this lucky time must be over. Pittsburgh as well, very dependent on steel industry lost 12,7% of its population in 1980-1990 alone, followed by a 9,5% decline in the next decade[34].

Nevertheless there is no city like Detroit, the only city that reached more than a million inhabitants, nearly two million and later shrunk below a million. *"Detroit has become a symbol of both the American Dream and the American Nightmare"*[35]. Unprecedented shrinkage followed unknown growth, when *The Big Three* Ford, GM and Chrysler, the dominant employers and driving force of the city got into trouble. In the decade from 1970 to 1980 alone, 208,000 jobs got lost[36] and still the unemployment is nearly three times the national average[37]. People either left the region or fled to the suburbs (see graphic).

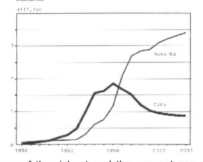

02 population development in the city of Detroit and suburbs

A development that also reinforced nationwide extreme racial segregation and led to a distribution of 78% Whites in the suburbs and 79% of black people in the inner city[38]. Another typical characteristic of shrinkage besides sub-urbanization is segregation in some cases across ethnical cleavages but more often across income. Detroit is very polarized in this regard containing some of the richest and the poorest communities in the U.S. The average monthly income of the city's inhabitants is $1055 compared to $1547 in the US and up to $2545 in some Detroit suburbs such as Oakland or Macomb with $1828[39]. Shrinkage has made the workers city Detroit much more unequal. The Detroit Almanac (2001) describes this polarization in the following way: *"On one block it looks like ground zero of the rust belt, the next like Jay Gatsby's front lawn. Burdened by an image of*

---

[34] Kingsley, G., Pettit, K. (2002)
[35] Cope, M. (2004). In: Shrinking Cities, Detroit (2004): 11
[36] Mende, D., Osswalt, P. (2004). In: Shrinking Cities, Detroit (2004): 3
[37] See: Cope, M. (2004). In: In: Shrinking Cities, Detroit (2004): 11
[38] Mende, D., Osswalt, P. (2004). In: Shrinking Cities, Detroit (2004): 3
[39] Booza, J. et al. (2004). In: Shrinking Cities, Detroit (2004): 7

_grime and crime, bigger than Madrid, Miami, Saigon and Sydney, beholden to a troubled recent past, metro Detroit is a tough place to figure out."[40]._

## 3.2. The East German case

Today what is considered to be the most pressing problem in Germany's urban development is how to handle the impact of demographic and economic decline. While discussing urban development in (East) Germany one should have in mind the special characteristics of this case, which limit possible generalization for other shrinking cities.

The most important special feature is that since the end of World War 2 East Germany, was a separate German state (GDR) under socialist governance until the Berlin Wall fell by the end of 1989. Since the GDR was founded it was always at danger of loosing its most qualified citizens to the West. This brain drain was one reason for building the famous wall-besides maintaining autocratic rule. After Germany became reunited the economic transformation from a planned to a free market economy had huge implications on one could say every aspect of life. In the Eastern countries (the "Länder") unemployment is still very significantly higher, productivity lower than in the Western part. Cities in the East did not only feel the huge economic challenges, often resulting in high unemployment and smaller tax bases. They were and are still confronted with a strong trend of sub urbanization and migration of citizens to the West. The graphic visualizes the dramatic population shrinkage in East German cities 1990-1997[41]. The housing and real estate market in the GDR as well as most aspects of city development were centrally planned and the government did not favor private houses and property. Since there was no free market allocation of supply and demand, several cities were planned or founded for a specific

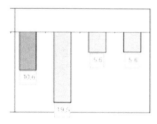

---

[40] The Detroit Almanac (2001). In: Shrinking Cities, Detroit (2004): 63
[41] Mäding, H. (2002)

economic purpose. High presence of military and a very big administration furthermore reduced incentives for cities to create jobs or economy friendly environments. Additionally free movement was limited so that city governments didn't gain much experience in attracting people.

Hoyerswerda for example was founded in 1956, as a model worker city to support the newly constructed biggest coal mines and refinery in Europe. Once the youngest city of the whole GDR in about 10 years it will be populated half by pensioners and has 18% unemployment today[42]. In the first years after reunification several hundred thousand citizens left East Germany for the West[43]. Not only the sheer number of citizens leaving their East German home cities presents a challenge also their structure, since usually the most qualified, young people leave: "*The population of most cities has fallen by 10% to 20%. Since 1980 the new Länder as a whole have lost about 6% of their population.*"[44].

Such an exodus of people has its unique historical causes but the effects for city development can be studied and generalized. It is striking that after Maribor in Slowenia the three cities in the European Union with the highest population loss are in East Germany: Halle, Frankfurt/Oder and Schwerin[45]. Shrinking East German cities such as the mentioned three are widely seen as predictors and negative scenarios for similar developments in parts of Western Germany. Under the guidance of the ministry for construction and traffic 16 West German cities foremost from former industrial centers such as Essen or Gelsenkirchen cooperate no longer to prevent the challenge of shrinking but to manage it[46].

The graphic[47] on the next page shows the population development in East Germany between 1990 and 1998. Dark blue shows a population loss greater 9%, lighter blue minus 6 to minus 9% and red marks different levels of population increase.

---

[42] Hannemann (2003)
[43] Mäding, H. (2002)
[44] Mäding, H. (2002)
[45] Eurostat (2004)
[46] Bundesministerium für Verkehr-, Bau-, und Wohnungswesen (2004)
[47] Bucher, H. (2001)

Two characteristics are important. First, nearly all districts suffer significant population losses, whereas most West German counties gain population.

Secondly all greater East German cities on the map, like Leipzig, Schwerin, Erfurt, Magdeburg etc. lost between 6 and more than 9% of their population, whereas their surrounding districts gained population. This can be best observed in the case of Berlin that lost and still looses population while the Hinterland gains.

The reasons for the shrinkage of a high number of East German cities are numerous. The main problem is the disappointing economic situation, leading to high unemployment and lower taxes. But also other factors play a big role such as rising sub-urbanization, unknown in the GDR and movement of especially younger people towards the West. Combined with decreasing fertility and low immigration, the East German cities are aging dramatically. The number of people under 18 years of age will for example decrease by 40% in only about 18 years and the urban-rural age disparities are severe: "*Agglomerations are older than rural regions, cities are older than their suburban areas*"[48]. Annex A6 shows how significantly East German cities will be aging as a result of migration and shrinkage. These cities are not without hope but they will have to adjust to a smaller scale.

## 4. What can be done?

Since there are a variety of reasons why cities shrink there can't be a silver bullet for the turnaround. Nevertheless, there are some quite typical patterns of shrinkage, which can be addressed besides the specific circumstances of each case. Cities that have relatively homogeneous neighbourhoods, for example just for workers of the

---

[48] Bucherer (2001)

local industry and a high dependency on very few companies/industries increase the risk of future shrinkage. Low immigration and fertility rate and therefore aging urban populations are other factors that speed up the shrinkage process. Since immigration and fertility rate are more influenced at the national level and are often overall demographic, socio-cultural trends this is hard to address by city governments. Besides aging (a natural decrease) there are two social factors leading to shrinkage. People either move away or they "just" move to suburbia. At city and at the national level one could decrease incentives for private homes in the green and increase incentives to renovate and invest in the old core of cities. A good public transportation system in the core of the city can function as an additional incentive as well as tax reductions and public goods such as libraries and parks concentrated in the center. It might be the case that the overall demographic trend will decrease sub urbanization and revitalize the inner city, since elderly might prefer short distances and centralized, fast supply with health care and other services.

US census data on city development as well as data on the German cases showed that turnarounds of cities, which were very dependent on single industries, are seldom and that decline processes are very sustainable often over several decades. Shrinkage is a hidden threat and needs long term and sustainable planning to be addressed effectively. Given that political business cycles of city government might be too short sighted to address such a long-term trend co-operation with local groups, NGOs and between cities should go without saying. A diverse economic base, though hard to achieve and young immigrants can be other factors to reduce the risk of shrinkage.

Suburbia made cities grow very significantly reduced city budgets when the suburbs grew beyond city borders often combined with a segregation of ethnic and income groups as in the case of Detroit. It is not an easy political process but cities, which suffer from citizens moving to suburbs instead of other places, could strive to enlarge city borders to include suburbia. A way *to prevent the polarized city"* as Leipzig mayor Tiefensee expresses it[49].

First citizens might be happy about low rents due to high vacancy rates (as in Leipzig or Detroit), since landlords also have to maintain the flats and apartments

---

[49] Tiefensee (2003)

they can't rent out, the achievable monthly rent might fall below a level of economic return and the whole housing market crashes. Here only demolishing buildings can be part of the solution. This in turn increases the number of vacant public places. Unused space and ruins, tall grass and an overall declining public sphere might lead to a nearly anti-urban, absurd picture: "*There were reports of people seeing coyotes prowling through the streets of what once had been thriving neighborhoods. Detroit, one urbanologist stated, was "past the point of no return*"[50]. An extreme way to address the vacant space in the inner cities might be to build a suburban like structure within the city core or to bring big sports facilities back to the city.

A well-known example for a successful turnaround is the city of Manchester and to a certain degree Liverpool. Both have been pioneering cities in the industrial age. Liverpool relied very much on its harbor and Manchester on textile and cotton manufacturing and UK´s relationship with India as major trade partner and market. The conditions of Manchesters working class inspired Karl Marx to write the Communist Manifesto and Manchester became a symbol of the Industrial age. The city growth was enormous and in the 1930s both cities peaked at around 900,000 inhabitants. The decline due to de-industrialization and the end of the colonial empire was even more astonishing and both cities until today lost about half their population[51]. Both cities show the typical signs of shrinking cities. Liverpool 2001 had more than 500 ha of vacant buildings, "*Unemployment soared to unimaginable heights*[52]", in both cities more than 18% of the population receive benefits, in 1995 unemployment in Manchester was 18,9% and there is a high (income) polarization between districts[53]. One could write long about the decline and shrinkage of Manchester but here for the purpose of the paper it is more relevant to examine why Manchester is well known for its exceptional turnaround.

Neither has Manchester gained much population nor has it become the industrial powerhouse it once was. Manchester today looks very differently from its past and "*With all it's contradictions, Manchester appears today as the 'fastest*

---

[50] Mirel, J. (1998): 240
[51] See: Shrinking cities (2004): 3f.
[52] Misslewitz, P. (2004). In: Shrinking Cities (2004): 115
[53] See: Shrinking cities (2004): 8, 33

*growing shrinking city' in the UK.*"[54]. The city government after long decades of city decline has accepted the change. The former size won't come back soon if it will be achieved at all and also the former economic base nowadays looks differently. Manchester shook off the image of decline through a variety of means. First the city is most known for the *"Rediscovery of the Warehouse"*. With the help of private-public-partnerships the new conservative government since the mid 80s replaced "municipal socialism" with "municipal entrepreneurialism"[55]. With an overall pro business approach and due to very low real estate prices and rents it was possible to develop the leisure, sports and cultural sector. A growing music industry, thriving bar and cultural scene and rising student numbers turned a lot of vacant warehouses and former factories into vital urban landscape: *"The last 15 years have seen Manchester emerge as the capital of successful regeneration, a model of how a city can re-invent itself through branding, self-promoting and re-building"*[56]. In the late 70s and early 80s the decline was most severely felt in the inner city, where less than 1000 inhabitants lived[57]. Manchester has very successfully addressed this typical decline of the inner city. On has to come from just administering the decline to managing the change. *"To the visitor, the booming city centre still appears as an island surrounded by a ring of de-industrialized wastelands and vacant and rundown estates ranking high on the national deprivation index."*[58]. So even the successful case of Manchester's return is a process of continuing change and active management.

The circumstances and challenges of Manchester's shrinkage might be specific in its causes and consequences. However Manchester has addressed typical challenges of shrinking cities and has created lessons learned for cities facing similar challenges. City management and the people of Manchester have not tried to re-establish old economic models of the industrial age but have looked for new opportunities. They could address shrinkage, aging and sub urbanization by focusing on the economy first, the city center, youth culture, the university and the leisure

---

[54] Misslewitz, P. (2004). In: Shrinking Cities (2004): 34
[55] Misslewitz, P. (2004). In: Shrinking Cities (2004): 33
[56] Misslewitz, P. (2004). In: Shrinking Cities (2004): 34
[57] Misslewitz, P. (2004). In: Shrinking Cities (2004): 33
[58] Misslewitz, P. (2004). In: Shrinking Cities (2004): 34

sector. Even though this still ongoing process took years it shows that shrinking cities can have a future.

## 5. Concluding Remarks

This paper aimed at showing that there is not only the phenomenon of increased urbanization, population growth and mega-cities, but also a big and growing trend and management challenge of shrinking cities.

The theories and circumstances for city growth and decline are numerous. However, from the various roles of a city such as religious, administrative centers and fortifications against enemies it's role, as market place seems to be the currently most important one. Market changes, de-industrialization, higher labor and capital mobility due to globalization provide an enormous growth opportunity for cities, but they also increase the risk of shrinkage for all cities that can't keep up with the speed of change. Demographic change leading to declining societies in the future will further increase shrinking. Nowadays Western city managers are most confronted with the problem of shrinking and its numerous consequences on the quality of life in their cities. People moving away to other places, sub urbanization and aging city centers are the major forms of shrinkage and the change of citizens' social structure.

When cities shrink also the public sphere is dying and decline processes are hard to stop. A statement on Detroit's decline is typical in this regard: "*The vast population decline in the city has created a scene that looks as if it never left the year 1968, kept in an eternal freeze frame, while nature grows over it.*"[59]. All the dynamism, high future expectations and vitality, of ever moving, never sleeping urban life slows down. Crime, unemployment and abandoned buildings are the most visible signs of this hidden challenge and 'freezing' process. Turnarounds such as the case of Manchester give hope that foresighted city management can give shrinking cities a future.

Shrinking has been fueled foremost by economic change and sub urbanization but in the future aging and declining populations will add a third factor to this problem.

---

[59] Cope, M. (2004). In: Shrinking Cities (2004): 11

Then aging China and today's youth bulge countries might learn of the Western experience with shrinking cities[60].

---

[60] A city such as Bejing for example already had 14% of elderly in 1997 and this figure is expected to increase to 30% by 2025. In: Li, Y (2005)

## References

1. Bairoch, P. (1988): Cities and Economic Development: From the Dawn of History to the Present. In: The Cities of Asia Socioeconomic Systems Differ from Those of Europe, Chicago: 349-365, 493-518
2. Berlin Institute for Population and Development (2004): Deutschland 2020. Die demografische Zukunft der Nation (Germany 2020. The demographic future of the nation). At: http://www.berlin-institut.org/index1.html
3. Bucher, H. (2001): Aging and depopulation of rural areas in Europe – the German example. At: http://www.iiasa.ac.at/Research/ERD/net/pdf/bucher_1.pdf
4. Bundesministerium für Verkehr-, Bau-, und Wohnungswesen (2004): Stadtumbau West. 16 Pilotstädte bauen um, Berlin.
5. Cohen, B. (2004): Small cities, big problems. At: http://www.issues.org/issues/20.3/realnumbers.html
6. Collins, L. (2003): Detroit is not alone. Can an art project help remedy global postindustrial decay? At: http://www.metrotimes.com/editorial/story.asp?id=5718
7. European Commission (2005): Flash Eurobarometer. Urban Audit Perception Survey. Local Perception sof Quality of Life in 31 European Cities. At: www.urbanaudit.org/UAPS%20leaflet.pdf
8. ECOSOC (2004): World Urbanization Prospects. The 2003 Revision. At: www.un.org/esa/population/ publications/wup2003/WUP2003Report.pdf
9. Eurostat (2005): Europe in figures. Eurostat Yearbook 2005, Luxembourg
10. Eurostat (2004): Urban Audit. Demographic, economic and social data on 258 cities across Europe. At: http://epp.eurostat.cec.eu.int/portal/page?_pageid=1073,46587259&_dad=portal&_schema=PORTAL&p_product_ code=3-25062004-BP
11. Flanagan,W. G. (1993): Contemporary Urban Sociology, New York
12. Hannemann, C. (2003): Schrumpfende Städte in Ostdeutschland- Ursachen und Folgen einer Stadtentwicklung ohne Wirtschaftswachstum. In: Politik und Zeitgeschichte, 28: 16-31
13. Holcim Foundation (2005): Holcim Forum for Sustainable Construction. At: www.holcimfoundation.org/media/ publications/firstforum/for_wk3.pdf
14. Kim, S. (2005): The rise and decline of U.S. urban densities.
15. Kingsley, G.T., Pettit, K.L. (2002): Population Growth and Decline in City Neighborhoods. Urban Institute Publication at: http://www.urban.org/url.cfm?ID=310594
16. League of Minessota cities' state (2004): Sate of the Cities Report 2004. At: http://www.lmnc.org/pdfs/SOTC04/sotc04chap4.pdf
17. Li, Y. (2005): The Challenges of Aging Toward Chinese Society. In: Public Administration and Management: An Interactive Journal, (10), 3,:25-45
18. Lupton, R., Power, A. (2004): The Growth and Decline of Cities and Regions. At: http://sticerd.lse.ac.uk/dps/case/cbcb/census1.pdf
19. Mäding, H. (2005): Schrumpfen ist keine Schande (Shrinking is no shame). At: http://www.difu.de/publikationen/difu-berichte/3_05/01.phtml
20. Mäding, H. (2002): Migration processes – Challenges for German Cities. Paper delivered at the Nordregio Conference "Spatial Development in Europe", Stockholm, 4 January 2002. At: German Institute for Urbanism: http://www.difu.de/english/occasional/migration-processes.shtml#1
21. Mirel, J. (1998): After the Fall : Continuity and Change in Detroit, 1981 – 1995. In: History of Education Quarterly, 38 (3):237-267
22. Mumford, L. (1956): The Natural History of Urbanization. In: http://habitat.aq.upm.es/boletin/n21/almum.en.html
23. Sadowski, A., et al (2003): Megacities: Trends and issues towards sustainable urban development. At: mc2000.arch.hku.hk/Megacities2000.pdf
24. Shrinking Cities, Detroit (2004): Working papers. Detroit. At: www.shrinkingcities.com
25. Shrinking Cities (2004). Working papers. Manchester/Liverpool. At: www.shrinkingcities.com/fileadmin/ shrink/downloads/pdfs/WP-II_Manchester_Liverpool.pdf
26. Tiefensee, W. (2003): Stadtentwicklung zwischen Schrumpfung und Wachstum. In: Politik und Zeitgeschichte, 28: 3-6
27. UN Press Release (2004): UN Report says world urban population of 3 billion today, expected to reach 5 billion by 2030. At: www.un.org/esa/population/ publications/wup2003/pop899_English.doc
28. U.S. Cenus Bureau (2004): Global Population at a Glance. 2002 and Beyond. At: http://www.census.gov/prod/2005pubs/p60-229.pdf

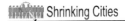 

29. U.S. Census Bureau (2004): Megacities map. At: www.census.gov/popest/archives/1990s/SU-map-9099.pdf

30. U.S. Department of Health and Human Service, U.S. Department of Commerce (2002): An Ageing W 2001. At: http://www.census.gov/prod/www/abs/popula.html

31. Vogel, S. (2005): How to fix a shrinking city? At: http://www.freep.com/cgi-bin/forms/printerfriendly.pl

32. Washington Post (2005): A shrinking New Orleans. At: http://www.washingtonpost.com/wp-dyn/content/article/2005/10/25/AR2005102501627.html

33. Wikipedia (01/2006): New Orleans. At: http://en.wikipedia.org/wiki/New_Orleans,_Louisiana

## Annexes

A1: Annual growth rate of global population

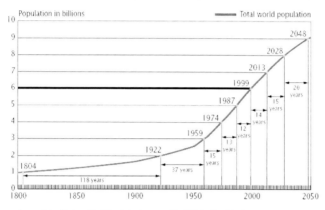

**Annual Additions and the Annual Growth Rate of Global Population**
The growth of global population has peaked.

Source: United Nations, *World Population Prospects: The 1994 Revision*; U.S. Census Bureau, International Programs Center, International Data Base and unpublished tables.

U.S. Census Bureau (2004): 1

A2: Percent aged 65 and over

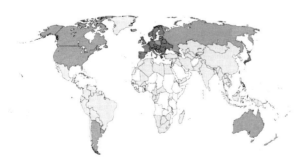

Figure 1-1
Percent Aged 65 and Over: 2000

US Census Bureau
(2001): 4

## A3: The World's 25 oldest countries 2000

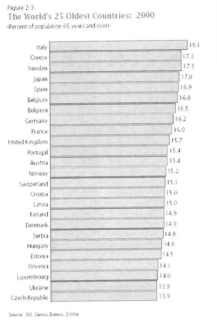

Figure 2-3.
The World's 25 Oldest Countries: 2000
(Percent of population 65 years and over)

| Country | Percent |
|---|---|
| Italy | 18.1 |
| Greece | 17.3 |
| Sweden | 17.3 |
| Japan | 17.0 |
| Spain | 16.9 |
| Belgium | 16.8 |
| Bulgaria | 16.5 |
| Germany | 16.2 |
| France | 16.0 |
| United Kingdom | 15.7 |
| Portugal | 15.4 |
| Austria | 15.4 |
| Norway | 15.2 |
| Switzerland | 15.1 |
| Croatia | 15.0 |
| Latvia | 15.0 |
| Finland | 14.9 |
| Denmark | 14.9 |
| Serbia | 14.8 |
| Hungary | 14.6 |
| Estonia | 14.5 |
| Slovenia | 14.1 |
| Luxembourg | 14.0 |
| Ukraine | 13.9 |
| Czech Republic | 13.9 |

Source: U.S. Census Bureau, 2000a.

U.S. Census (2001): 10

## A4: Fertility rate in the EU-25

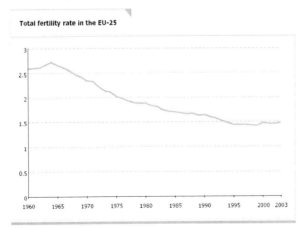

**Total fertility rate in the EU-25**

Eurostat (2005): 71

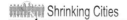 Shrinking Cities

A5: Eurostat: Annual average population change 1996-2001

| The ten highest | | | The ten lowest | | |
|---|---|---|---|---|---|
| ES | Palma de Mallorca | 2.6% | SI | Maribor | -3.1% |
| ES | Pamplona/Iruña | 2.3% | DE | Halle an der Saale | -3.0% |
| ES | Badajoz | 2.2% | DE | Frankfurt (Oder) | -2.7% |
| FI | Oulu | 2.0% | DE | Schwerin | -2.7% |
| PT | Braga | 1.5% | RO | Bacau | -2.4% |
| CY | Lefkosia | 1.3% | DE | Magdeburg | -2.3% |
| FI | Tampere | 1.2% | RO | Cluj-Napoca | -2.2% |
| ES | Logroño | 1.2% | RO | Piatra Neamt | -2.0% |
| ES | Murcia | 1.2% | RO | Targu Mures | -1.8% |
| UK | Inner London | 1.1% | IT | Venezia | -1.6% |

Eurostat (2004) : Urban Audit

A6 : Population dynamics of broad age groups in East Germany

## urban

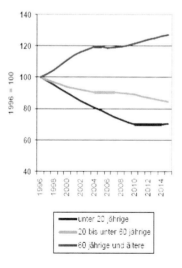

Bucherer, H. (2001)

28